PORTRAIT OF A SYMPHONY

PORTRAIT OF A SYMPHONY

TEXT & PHOTOGRAPHS BY
CONSTANTINE MANOS

FOREWORD BY AARON COPLAND

Publishers BASIC BOOKS, INC. *New York*

Published by Basic Books, Inc., New York
Library of Congress Catalog Card Number: 60-13144

PRINTED IN ITALY BY SHEET-FED GRAVURE
UNDER THE SUPERVISION OF CHANTICLEER PRESS, N.Y.C.

FOREWORD *by Aaron Copland*

HAVE YOU EVER BEEN a lone listener in the presence of a live symphony orchestra? Have you ever had the experience of hearing a hundred men perform for yourself alone? I boast of having been that lucky: composers who wait patiently to hear their own work rehearsed may occasionally find the auditorium emptied of all listeners but themselves. Without their being aware of it, more than one orchestra has played for me alone. Each such experience remains in my mind as a rare treat.

An equivalent treat awaits the viewer who turns the pages of this book of photographs. Here too, it seems to me, one may enjoy the vicarious pleasure of finding oneself, like the composer, alone in the presence of a great orchestra.

Think for a moment what a full-fledged orchestra is. This disparate conglomeration of personalities and talents is truly an entity like a nation; it is a living thing that breathes and moves in ways peculiar to its own being. At its head is a leader who, through bodily gestures and facial expressivity, acts out the music's progress. There are subtle understandings between leader and instrumentalists, psychological adjustments be-tween player and player, or section and section, all intent on achieving a single goal—the illumination of the composer's thought.

An orchestra is fully aware of its own power. It knows it can be awe-inspiring and nerve shattering, enraged and inconsolable, and then as suddenly melt us with a dulcet and almost feminine grace.

To the real *aficionado*, any aspect of an orchestra's activity is of interest. The backstage preparations, the drama of the tuning room, the gossip of the corridors, the gathering of the audience out front—these are the mundane scenes that balance and accompany the more brilliant action. Everyone from the ticket-taker to the man who encases the harp for the night is charged with the glamour of an orchestra.

Of all our symphony orchestras, the one that has the most glamour for me is the one that makes its home in Symphony Hall. For thirty-five years I have seen the musical development of our age mirrored in their playing. I count myself among the many thousands of their admirers who will have much joy from possessing these visual impressions of this great orchestra.

THE BOSTON TRADITION

LIKE THE HUMAN PERSONALITY, that of a symphony orchestra is the sum of its experiences and environment.

Since its inception in 1881 the Boston Symphony Orchestra has been profoundly influenced by both. Its conductors and musicians, representing various schools of thought and performance, have provided the molding experiences from within. Cultural Boston and the particular audience it provides have had an exterior influence on the orchestra's development; the orchestra in turn has shaped its audience.

From the beginning the orchestra has felt the stamp of the strong Yankee individuals who have guided its growth. It was founded by Henry Lee Higginson of Boston, who as a music student in Vienna had heard the symphonies of Beethoven, Mozart, and Schubert played as they should be. Returning to Boston, he spent his fortune and devoted his lifetime to building an orchestra equal to the finest of Europe.

Gathering together the best musicians he could obtain at home and abroad, Mr. Higginson chose a German, Georg Henschel, as the first conductor. From its inception until 1918 the orchestra was ruled by a series of conductors schooled in the German tradition. After Henschel there followed Wilhelm Gericke (1881–1889, 1898–1906), Emil Paur (1893–1898), Arthur Nikisch (1889–1893), Max Fiedler (1908–1912), and Karl Muck (1906–1908, 1912–1918).

The First World War marked the end of an era. In 1918 Mr. Higginson turned his gift of one symphony orchestra over to the people of Boston. The newly formed Board of Trustees engaged Henri Rabaud from Paris, beginning the French influence which has since been especially felt in the woodwinds.

The following year Pierre Monteux first came to Boston and virtually rebuilt the orchestra. Musicians were no longer imported from Central Europe, and the contingent of native talent increased as America became a music conscious and musically proficient nation. With Monteux at the helm Bostonians also heard the new sounds of Stravinsky or Ravel and began developing that open-minded receptiveness which has made traditionally conservative Boston a fertile field for new music.

This championing of new music continued with Serge Koussevitzky, who became a legend in the twenty-five years he reigned over the orchestra. Koussevitzky championed little-known composers now universally recognized. Under Koussevitzky the orchestra achieved heights of brilliance in an era that saw Stokowski in Philadelphia and Toscanini in New York. When Koussevitzky retired in 1950, the choice of his successor proved another happy one.

Under the leadership of Charles Munch the orchestra has won international acclaim, touring Europe and the Far East for the first time, and attracting greater audiences at its summer festival at Tanglewood. The new audience it has reached through recordings, radio, and television is immense; in 1959 it broadcast the first live orchestral concert to Europe over the trans-Atlantic cable.

Although the orchestra belongs to the world by now, Bostonians still think of it as a local institution all their own. Certainly they have a right to feel this way, for they have consistently filled Symphony Hall every season since it was built in 1900. It is an audience that knows its orchestra so well that it has assumed the proportions of a great silent critic whose standards are based on many lifetimes of attentive hearings.

Both musicians and conductors in Boston have felt the presence of their audience through the years. They know from the ovations they receive abroad that what is good enough for Boston is good enough for the world.

SYMPHONY . . . a harmony of dedicated men, fusing their talents with a tradition of eighty years. The living instrument: one hundred four musicians and their conductor. Their repertoire: unlimited and profound. Their audience: devoted, receptive, critical. Their home: a staid temple dedicated to music and built for the orchestra in 1900. Their address: Symphony Hall, Boston.

THE MUSICIANS . . . each man bringing to the orchestra his talent and the fruits of his lone labor; each carefully chosen not only for his skill but also for his compatibility within the ensemble; each a part of the collaboration, yet retaining his own individual sound—all tones together making the tone of the orchestra. Their names are as varied as the sounds they produce: Knudson, Bielski, Pappoutsakis, Gibson, Resnikoff, Silverstein, Cardillo, Hoherman, Smith. They come from Warsaw, Cleveland, Cairo, Brooklyn, Berlin. And from the grass roots of America: Marlow, Oklahoma; Alpha, Illinois; Rumford, Maine. Many are great teachers and, true to tradition, students of great masters— Joachim, Ysaye, Hubay, Auer. There are old-timers: Einar Hansen; born in Copenhagen, product of the Hamburg Conservatory, a member of the violin section for thirty-four years. And the products of the younger American tradition: Alfred Schneider; born in St. Louis, graduate of the Eastman School of Music, with the orchestra five years.

THE CONDUCTOR . . . a scholar, a fine musician, a wise leader,
he is the arbiter of sound and interpretation. Upon his shoulders lies
the artistic burden and joy of realizing the scores of Beethoven, Bach,
Mozart. Molding one hundred four musicians into a single instrument,
he draws from that instrument the most beautiful sound it can produce.
He is firm and demanding, yet considerate. Above all he is humble before
the music and modest before the world. He is Charles Munch, a
Frenchman born in Strasbourg and reared on Bach. He knows his
instrument, the orchestra, from within. He was in his middle forties,
concertmaster of the famed Gewandhaus Orchestra in Leipzig, when he
put away his violin for the baton. He had played under Furtwängler and
other great conductors; he is now a part of that tradition.

Haydn		Isola overt.
HAYDN		SYMPHONY 28
HAYDN	866 'HORN SIGNAL'	SYMPHONY 31
HAYDN	489 'FAREWELL'	SYMPHONY 45
HAYDN	684 'THE QUEEN'	SYMPHONY 85
HAYDN	'IMPERIAL'	SYMPHONY 53
HAYDN	436 'THE HUNT'	SYMPHONY 73
HAYDN	200 'THE BEAR'	SYMPHONY 82
HAYDN	65 E	SYMPHONY 86
HAYDN	245 A	SYMPHONY 88
HAYDN	436	SYMPHONY 90
HAYDN	152 'OXFORD'	SYMPHONY 92
HAYDN	64	SYMPHONY 93
HAYDN	65 F 'SURPRISE'	SYMPHONY 94
HAYDN	65	SYMPHONY 95

THE REPERTOIRE... a corner of the orchestra's library. Here, in one thousand six hundred scores, is a treasury of Western man's musical heritage. Here are the venerated European editions of the old masters as well as contemporary manuscripts that have the test of time still before them. This is the fountainhead of the orchestra, the vital link between composition and performance. The conductor chooses, the music appears on the stands, and a hundred talents transform the mathematical perfection of thousands of tiny black notes into living music.

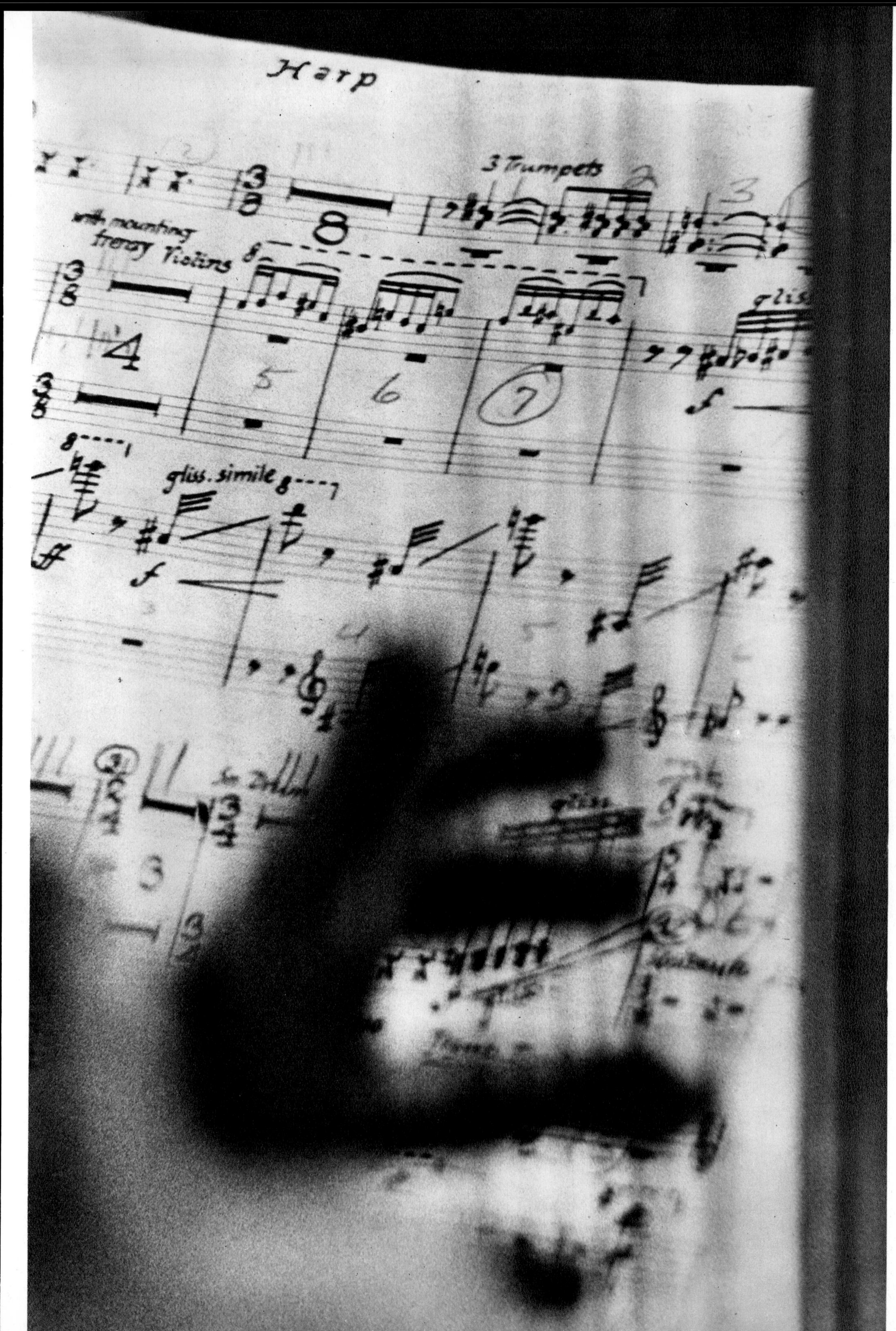
Harp
3 Trumpets
with mounting frenzy Violins
gliss. simile

THE AUDIENCE . . . some Bostonians have owned the same seat
in Symphony Hall for fifty years. They are often the first to arrive for a
concert, sitting quietly in the dim stillness waiting for the Hall to
come to life around them. Many of them first came to "Symphony" as
children and still remember the wonder of that experience. Time is the
difference between fascination and devotion. This is the process which has
brought the Orchestra a devoted following and made Symphony Hall a
temple and a landmark.

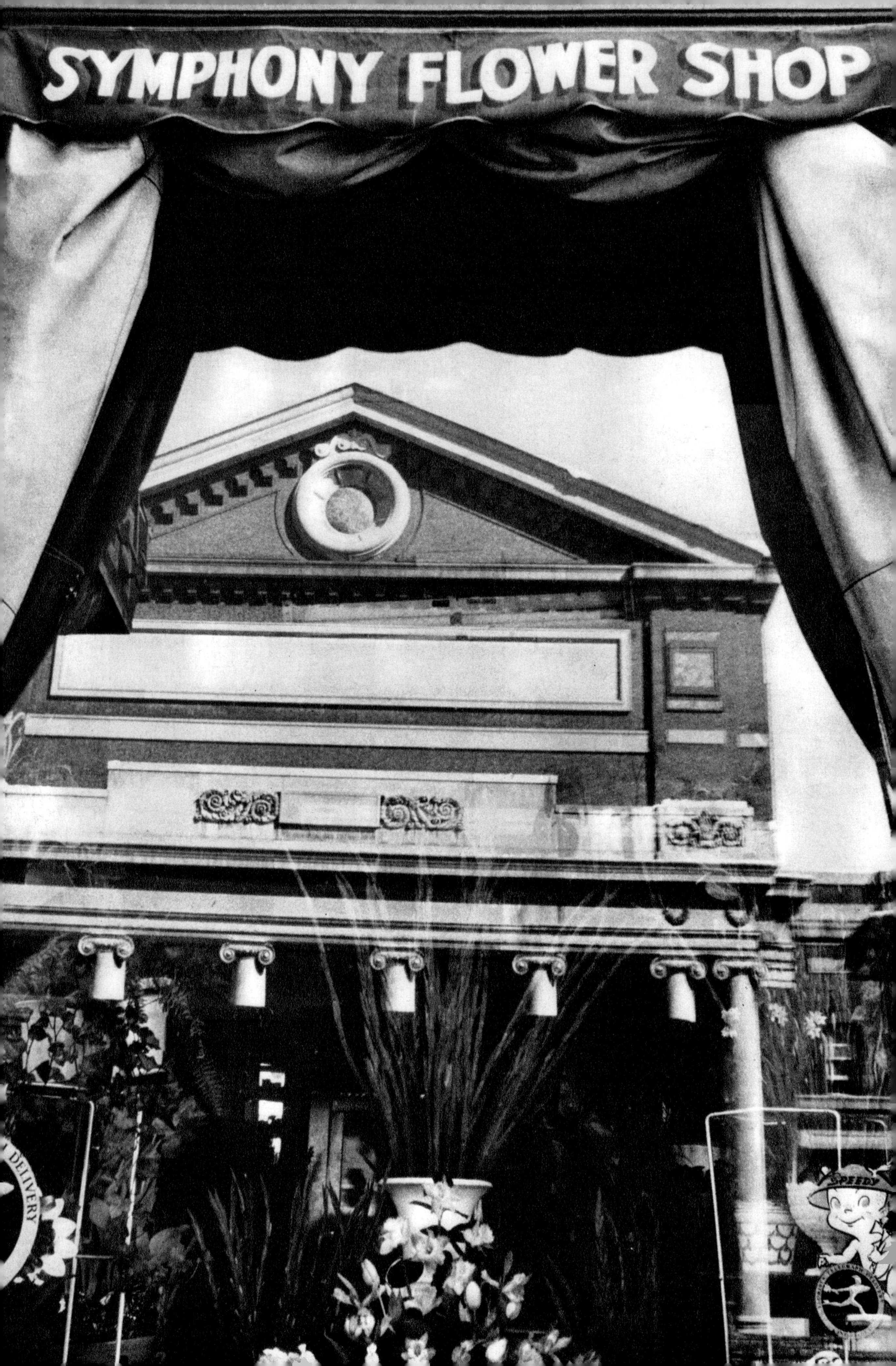
SYMPHONY FLOWER SHOP
DELIVERY
SPEEDY

Symphony TAILOR SHOP

ATTENTION
Don't THROW Away
DOUBLE BREASTED SUITS.
We can Restyle Your
DOUBLE-BREASTED to SINGLE-BREASTED

SYMPHONY RD.

SYMPHONY

SHELTER
AREA

SINGLE
CAR
STOP

FALMOUTH ST - M
HUNTINGTON AV

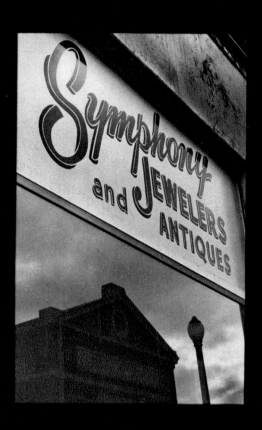

Symphony
JEWELERS
and
ANTIQUES

Symphony SANDWICH SHOP

DELICATESSEN TO TAKE OUT

DELICATESSEN

THE WARMUP... on a wintry evening, as the first lights go on and long before the audience arrives, musicians are warming up their instruments and limbering cold fingers. On stage in the silence of the empty hall the harpist gently plucks his instrument into tune. Dormant instruments are taken from wall lockers backstage; street clothes are exchanged for the somber blacks and starched whites of the concert stage. A few card games are in progress and small clusters of musicians chat to the subdued accompaniment of their own music. The cellist makes a minute adjustment on his bridge; the tuba player breathes life into cold plumbing; the oboist repairs delicate mechanism. Like them, the majority of the musicians will eventually seek the solitude of a quiet corner, for this is the time when old friends, the musician and his instrument, become one again.

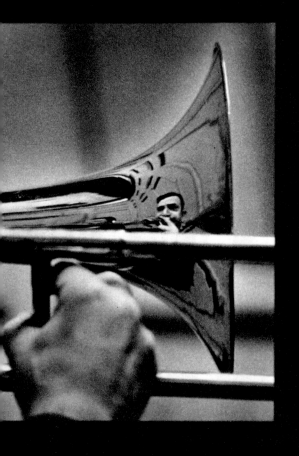

5
BSO
6
PROP
BSO
BOSTON SYMPHONY ORCH.
SYMPHONY HALL
BOSTON, MASS.

FESTIVAL . . . in the summer the music-makers trade their somber winter formals for cool whites and retreat to their home at Tanglewood in the Berkshire hills. In the informal atmosphere of the great shed they play for six thousand; often an equal number gathers leisurely on the surrounding lawns. Great music knows no season and its disciples come from the four corners of the earth.

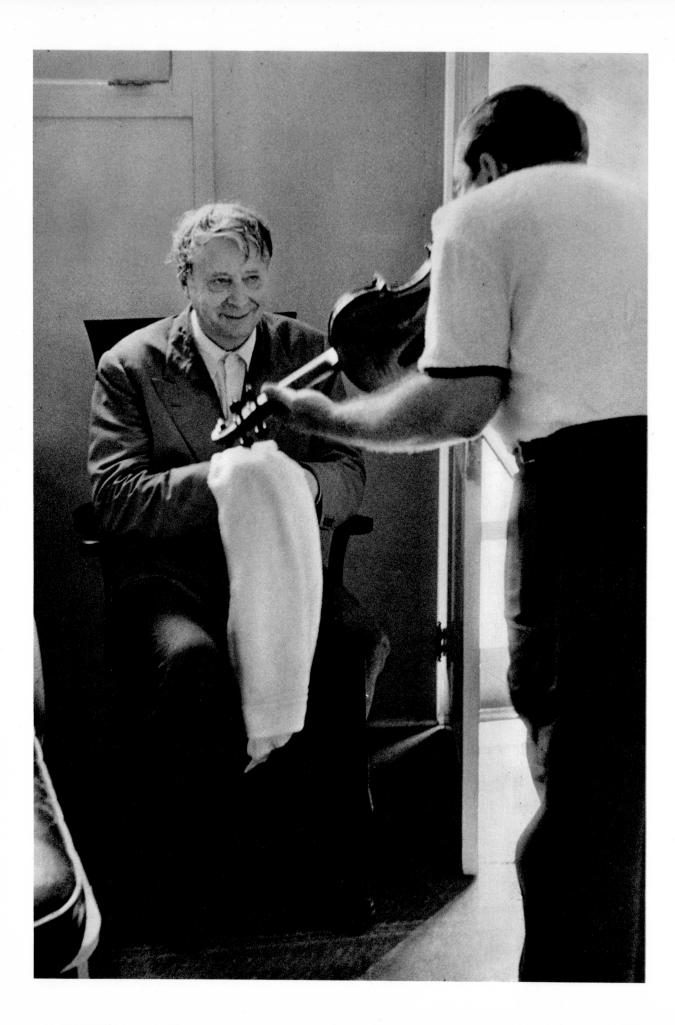

THE HONORED GUESTS . . . artistic collaboration in the concert hall gives birth to those evenings of inspired music making that are not soon forgotten. There is the anticipation of seeing the new and younger talents for the first time. There are the elder statesmen of music, who join their consummate art with that of the orchestra in those rare performances that hold an audience spellbound and leave them stunned. Here are some of these men of music: Copland, Istomin, Casals, Serkin, Monteux, Piatigorsky, Steinberg, Schippers, Barbirolli.

COPLAND

MONTEUX

SCHIPPERS

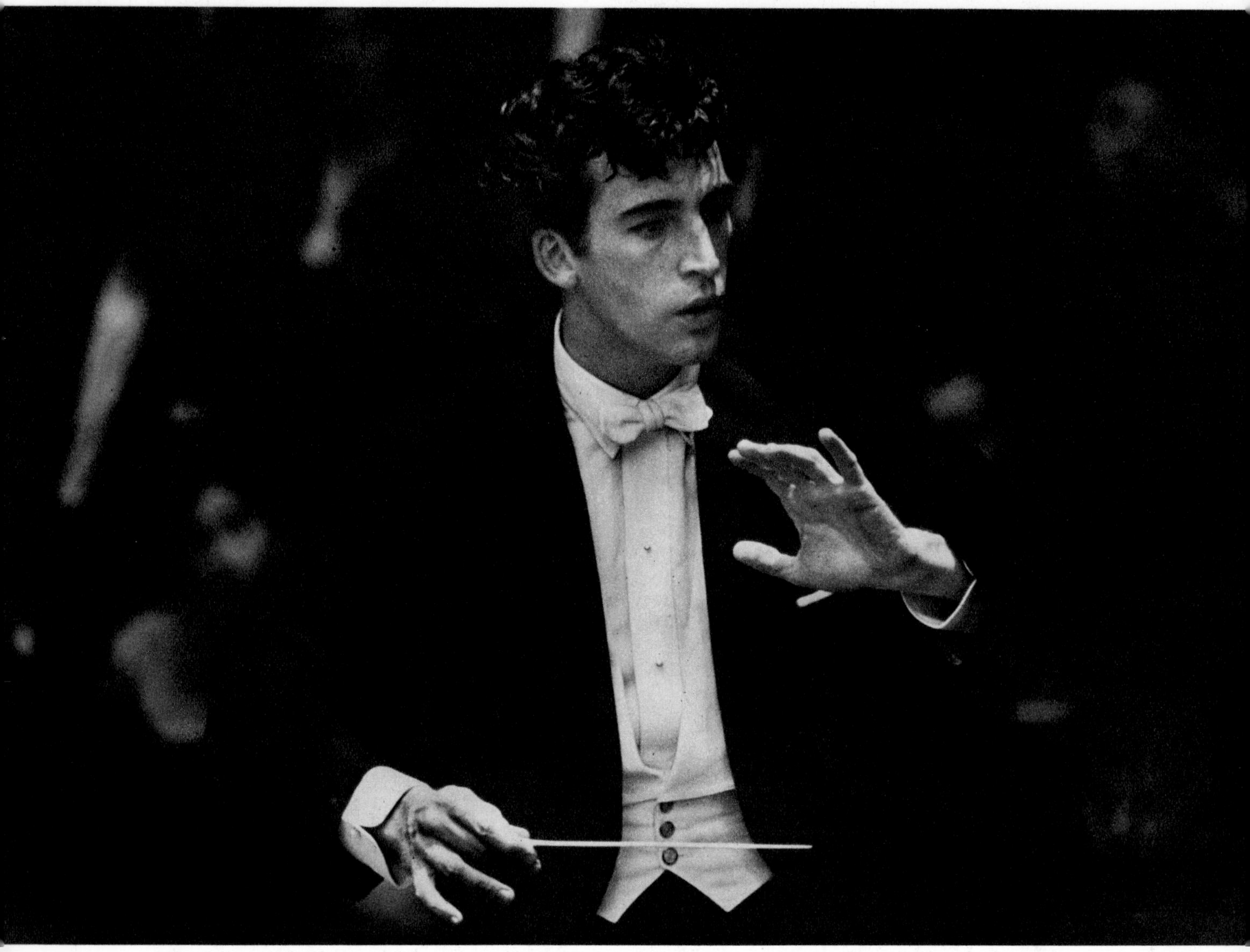

BARBIROLLI

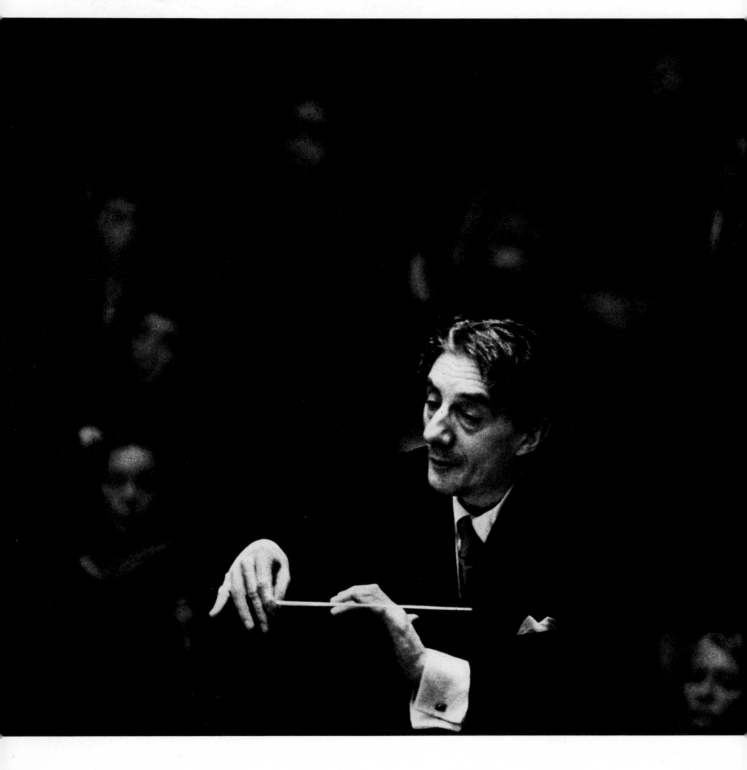

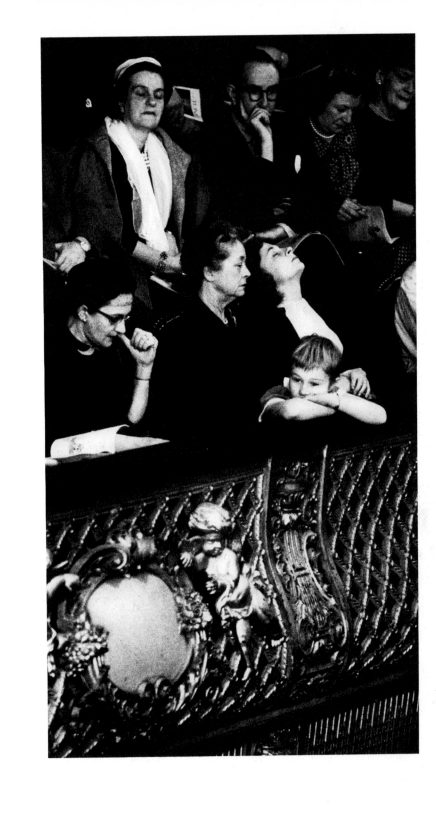

MUSIC FOR POSTERITY ... the orchestra is performing
behind locked doors, and there is no audience in the hall. Through the
electronic media of microphone, tape, and disc the orchestra is reaching
out to millions who may never see it. On occasion a great artist like
Heifetz may come to record a concerto. After each session the performers
retire to the listening room to brood critically over the sounds they have
set down for posterity.

CATHEDRAL OF SOUND... the symphony orchestra is the culmination of man's search for perfection in the arts of musical composition and performance and in the craft of fine instrument making. The search found expression in the workshops of eighteenth-century Italian violin makers and continues with crafters of flutes in Boston, oboes in Paris, bassoons in Wiesbaden. The graceful curves of the string bass derive from the plaintive viols of the Middle Ages; the near-perfect flute of today was being developed on the banks of the Nile three thousand years ago. The composer's art began with the Greeks before Christ was born, and the performer's art began with man. In the orchestra, hundreds of sensitive fingers move surely and swiftly over strings and keys. There are the miniature crafts which each fine musician must apply to his own instrument to achieve beauty of tone, nuance of sound, perfect pitch: carving a paper thin bassoon reed from bamboo; muting the tone of a horn with a cupped palm; testing

the pitch of the snare drum with the mere brush of a finger. This is the tracery of the orchestra. Add the buttresses of the massed sounds of the various sections. Top this cathedral of sound with the conductor's art and watch the interplay of the individuals, the ensemble, and the whole. You are witnessing one of man's greatest achievements.

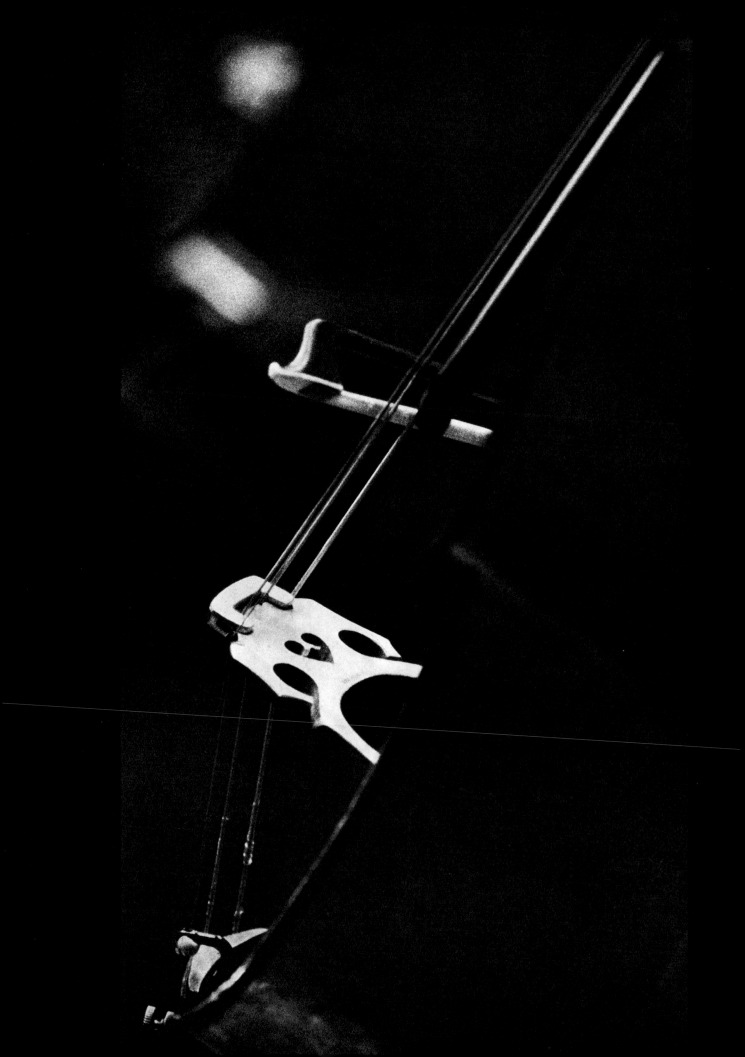

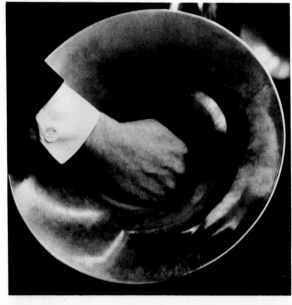

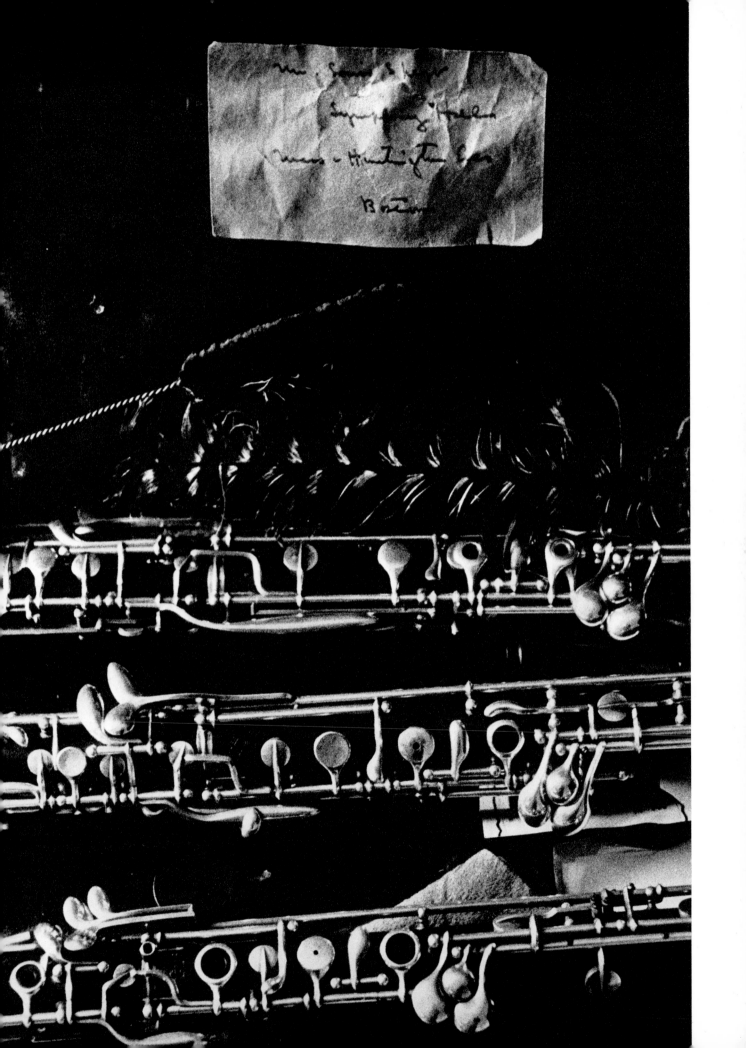

Boston Symphony Orchestra

CHARLES MUNCH, *Music Director*

RICHARD BURGIN, *Associate Conductor*

PERSONNEL

VIOLINS
Richard Burgin
Concert-master
Alfred Krips
George Zazofsky
Rolland Tapley
Joseph Silverstein
Vladimir Resnikoff
Harry Dickson
Gottfried Wilfinger
Einar Hansen
Joseph Leibovici
Emil Kornsand
Roger Shermont
Minot Beale
Herman Silberman
Stanley Benson
Leo Panasevich
Sheldon Rotenberg
Fredy Ostrovsky
Noah Bielski

Clarence Knudson
Pierre Mayer
Manuel Zung
Samuel Diamond
William Marshall
Leonard Moss
William Waterhouse
Alfred Schneider
Victor Manusevitch
Laszlo Nagy
Ayrton Pinto
Michel Sasson
Lloyd Stonestreet
Saverio Messina
Melvin Bryant

VIOLAS
Joseph de Pasquale
Jean Cauhapé
Eugen Lehner
Albert Bernard
George Humphrey
Jerome Lipson
Robert Karol
Reuben Green
Bernard Kadinoff
Vincent Mauricci
John Fiasca
Earl Hedberg

CELLOS
Samuel Mayes
Alfred Zighera
Jacobus Langendoen
Mischa Nieland
Karl Zeise
Martin Hoherman
Bernard Parronchi
Richard Kapuscinski
Robert Ripley
Winifred Winograd
Louis Berger
John Sant Ambrogio

BASSES
Georges Moleux
Henry Freeman
Irving Frankel
Henry Portnoi
Henri Girard
John Barwicki
Leslie Martin
Ortiz Walton

FLUTES
Doriot Anthony Dwyer
James Pappoutsakis
Phillip Kaplan

PICCOLO
George Madsen

OBOES
Ralph Gomberg
Jean de Vergie
John Holmes

ENGLISH HORN
Louis Speyer

CLARINETS
Gino Cioffi
Manuel Valerio
Pasquale Cardillo
Eb Clarinet

BASS CLARINET
Rosario Mazzeo

BASSOONS
Sherman Walt
Ernst Panenka
Theodore Brewster

CONTRA BASSOON
Richard Plaster

HORNS
James Stagliano
Charles Yancich
Harry Shapiro
Harold Meek
Paul Keaney
Osbourne McConathy

TRUMPETS
Roger Voisin
Armando Ghitalla
André Come
Gerard Goguen

TROMBONES
William Gibson
William Moyer
Kauko Kahila
Josef Orosz

TUBA
K. Vinal Smith

TIMPANI
Everett Firth
Harold Farberman

PERCUSSION
Charles Smith
Harold Thompson
Arthur Press

HARPS
Bernard Zighera
Olivia Luetcke

PIANO
Bernard Zighera

LIBRARY
Victor Alpert
William Shisler

THOMAS D. PERRY, JR., *Manager*